Pachyrhinosaurus
PAK-ee-rye-no-saw-russ

Triceratops
try-SER-a-tops

Micropachycephalosaurus
mike-row-pak-ee-SEF-a-la-saw-russ

Saltopus
SALT-o-pus

Teratosaurus
ter-AT-a-saw-russ

Protoceratops
pro-toe-SER-a-tops

Dilophosaurus
dye-LO-fa-saw-russ

Camarasaurus
KAM-a-ra-saw-russ

Scutellosaurus
scoo-TELL-o-saw-russ

Spinosaurus
SPY-na-saw-russ

Psittacosaurus
SIT-a-ka-saw-russ

Ouranosaurus
our-AN-a-saw-russ

To CAROLYN!

Bernard Moot 1991

A Dinosaur Named after Me

by Bernard Most

Harcourt Brace Jovanovich, Publishers

San Diego   New York   London

HBJ

Copyright © 1991 by Bernard Most

The author wishes to acknowledge the following books as sources
for the factual information contained in the text:
A Field Guide to Dinosaurs by David Lambert
The Illustrated Dinosaur Dictionary by Helen Roney Sattler
Dinosaur Dictionary by Donald F. Glut

Library of Congress Cataloging-in-Publication Data
Most, Bernard.
    A dinosaur named after me/by Bernard Most.—1st ed.
      p.   cm.
    Summary: Draws parallels between the physical characteristics and
  capabilities of particular dinosaurs and specific children and
  incorporates the name of each child into that of the dinosaur.
    ISBN 0-15-223494-2
    1. Dinosaurs—Juvenile literature.   [1. Dinosaurs.]   I. Title.
  QE862.D5M693   1991
  567.9'1—dc20   90-36272

First edition
A B C D E

The illustrations in this book were done in Pantone markers
on Bainbridge board 172, hot press finish.
Composition by TypeLink, Inc., San Diego, California
Color separations were made by Bright Arts, Ltd., Singapore
Printed and bound by Tien Wah Press, Singapore
Production supervision by Warren Wallerstein and Ginger Boyer
Designed by Alex P. Mendoza

To HBJ's very own DIANE-osaur,
my editor, Diane D'Andrade

Apatosaurus (ah-PAT-a-saw-russ)

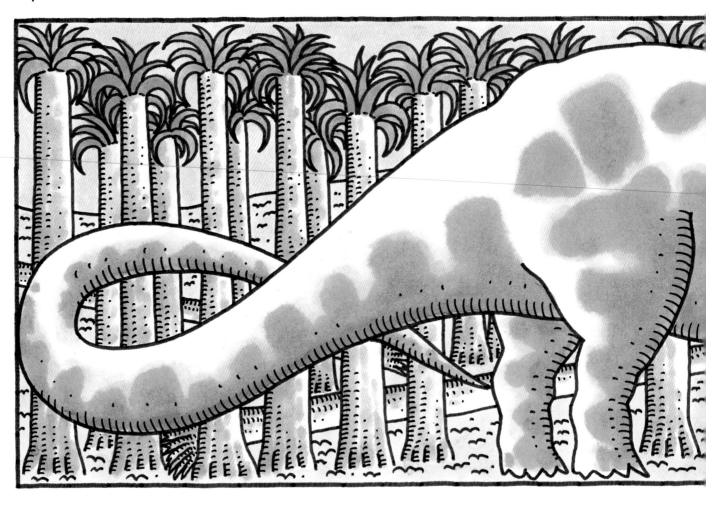

My favorite dinosaur is Apatosaurus.
This is the correct scientific name
for Brontosaurus, which was
thought to be a new dinosaur
when it was discovered.
But scientists now think it
is the same as a dinosaur
discovered years earlier,
Apatosaurus. I like the name
A-PAT-osaurus much
better anyway.

Pat

Brontosaurus (BRON-ta-saw-russ)

Ron

My favorite dinosaur is Brontosaurus. Everyone knows this dinosaur as Brontosaurus—so why change it? Many scientists today think dinosaurs were more like mammals and birds than reptiles. But no one wants to change the name *dinosaur,* which means "terrible lizard." If you must change the name of Brontosaurus, call it RON-tosaurus!

Pentaceratops (PEN-ta-ser-a-tops)

My favorite dinosaur was Triceratops . . . until I read about Pentaceratops. Its name means "five-horned face" because it had two more horns than Triceratops. It also had a much larger frill. Since I was born on the fifth day of the fifth month, five is my lucky number. This dinosaur should be named BEN-taceratops!

Ben

Anodontosaurus (an-a-dont-a-SAW-russ)

My favorite dinosaur is Anodontosaurus. This armored dinosaur's name means "toothless lizard" because its jaw was discovered without any teeth. I was reading about this dinosaur with my grandma. Because I'm losing my baby teeth, she said she would call this dinosaur ANDREW-dontosaurus.

Andrew

Iguanodon (ig-WAN-a-don)

My favorite dinosaur is Iguanodon.
This plant eater is always pictured with its
big spiky thumbs pointed up.
Scientists think it used its spiky thumbs
to defend against meat eaters.
Nobody does a better imitation of
one than I do. Would you dare
to shake hands with
Iguano-DAN?

Dan

Yaleosaurus (YALE-ee-a-saw-russ)

My favorite dinosaur is Yaleosaurus. It was named after Yale University because its fossils were found near the school. Yale's museum has a great dinosaur collection. When I grow up, I want to be a student at Yale and learn so much about this dinosaur they will rename it GAIL-eosaurus!

Gail

Aristosuchus (a-RISS-ta-sook-uss)

My favorite dinosaur is Aristosuchus.
Scientists first thought this meat eater's fossils were
from a crocodile, so they named
it "best crocodile." I love
reading about crocodiles
and dinosaurs. But if I
discover a dinosaur
that reminds me of a
crocodile, I will name it
CHRIS-tosuchus!

Chris

Brachiosaurus (BRAK-ee-a-saw-russ)

My favorite dinosaur is Brachiosaurus. It was a member of the tallest dinosaur family and could reach higher than any other dinosaur. I am the tallest person in my class, and I can reach higher than anybody. I would have named Brachiosaurus after me: ZACH-iosaurus.

Zach

Lambeosaurus (LAM-bay-a-saw-russ)

My favorite dinosaur is Lambeosaurus.
Scientists think it made loud, trumpet-
like sounds with its hollow crest.
When I play my trumpet, I close my
eyes and wonder if I sound anything
like this dinosaur. Was I surprised to
find out its other scientific name is
STEPHAN-osaurus!

Stephan

Ankylosaurus (an-KILE-a-saw-russ)

My favorite dinosaur is Ankylosaurus. Rows of bony plates and a clublike tail protected this peaceful plant eater from meat eaters. Every time I visit the museum and see a knight's armor, I think about this largest armored dinosaur. But a much better name would be HANK-ylosaurus!

Hank

Microvenator (mike-row-ven-AY-tor)

My favorite dinosaur is Microvenator, or "small hunter." This turkey-sized meat eater was good at catching its dinner because it was very fast and had grasping claws. I'm a small hunter, too. I'm good at catching my friends when we play hide-and-seek. "Ready or not, here comes MIKE-rovenator!"

Ready or not, here I come!

Mike

Maiasaura (my-a-SAW-ra)

My favorite dinosaur is Maiasaura.
Named "good mother lizard" because it was
found near a nest with fifteen baby
dinosaurs, scientists think it brought
food to its babies and took good
care of them. Mom says I take good
care of my baby brother. She says
this dinosaur's name should be
MARY-asaura.

Mary

Stegosaurus (STEG-a-saw-russ)

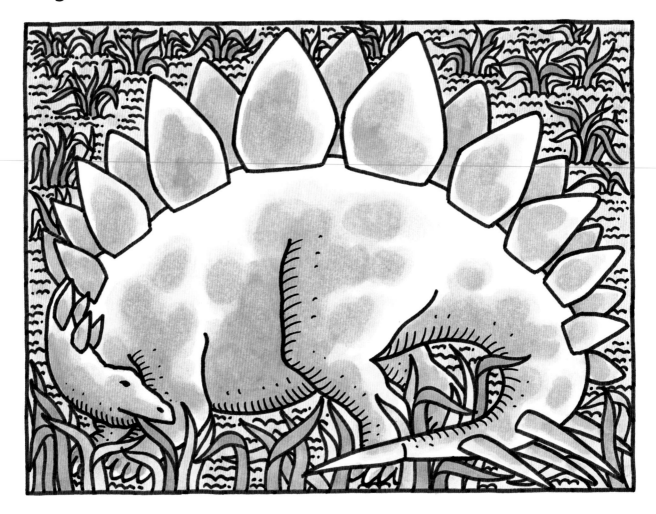

My favorite dinosaur is Stegosaurus.
Scientists think the large plates that covered
its back were for protection and made
Stegosaurus look larger to meat-eating
dinosaurs—just like my shoulder
pads protect me and make me look
larger to opposing teams.
My friends renamed Stegosaurus
GREG-osaurus.

Greg

Dravidosaurus (dra-VID-a-saw-russ)

David

My favorite dinosaur is Dravidosaurus. It was a member of the Stegosaurus family but one of the littlest, only ten feet long. It's like a little brother to Stegosaurus. I'm Greg's little brother, so if they change Stegosaurus to GREG-osaurus, I hope they change Dravidosaurus to DAVID-osaurus!

Avimimus (a-vee-MY-muss)

My favorite dinosaur is Avimimus. There was much that was birdlike about this little insect eater with feathered wings. Some scientists think modern birds evolved from dinosaurs. I would like to help prove that birds are living dinosaurs so they could rename this dinosaur AMY-mimus.

Amy

Tyrannosaurus Rex (tie-RAN-a-saw-russ REX)

My favorite dinosaur is Tyrannosaurus Rex,
the biggest, meanest, fiercest,
most powerful meat eater ever found.
It had teeth like giant knives.
Scientists named it "king of
the tyrant lizards."
Sometimes, when I have
a bad day or lose my temper,
my dad calls me
RYAN-osaurus Rex!

Ryan

Macrurosaurus (mak-ROO-ra-saw-russ)

My favorite dinosaur is Macrurosaurus, named "long-tailed lizard" because all they found of it were forty tailbones miles apart. They think this long tail belonged to a four-legged plant eater. That gave me an idea for a dinosaur game. I call it "Pin the tail on MARK-rurosaurus."

Mark

Kentrosaurus (KEN-tra-saw-russ)

My favorite dinosaur is KEN-trosaurus.
This "pointed lizard" had spikes
running from the top of its head
to the tip of its tail. That's why
I love drawing this dinosaur.
My friend Glenn says it would
be his favorite if it were
renamed GLENN-trosaurus.
But I like its name just the way it is.

Ken

Ornithomimus (orn-ith-a-MY-muss)

My favorite dinosaur is Ornithomimus.
It belonged to the "ostrich dinosaur" family,
the fastest dinosaurs. Scientists think
they ran even faster than modern
racehorses. I'm so fast, someday
I'm going to win a gold medal
in the Olympics. Then they could
name the fastest dinosaur
ANN-ithomimus.

Ann

Ammosaurus (AM-a-saw-russ)

My favorite dinosaur is Ammosaurus.
Its name means "sand lizard" because
of where its fossils were found. My
brother calls me sand lizard
because I like to play in the
sand so much. He says they should
change this dinosaur's name
from Ammosaurus to
SAM-osaurus.

Sam

Pterodactylus (ter-a-DAK-tie-luss)

My favorite is not a dinosaur.
It's Pterodactylus, a flying cousin of dinosaurs.
Some pterodactyls were tiny, like sparrows.
Others were much bigger, like hawks.
Scientists think they caught
insects in the air. I made my own
Pterodactylus kite. It's a
TERRY-dactylus!

Terry

Parasaurolophus (par-a-saw-ROL-a-fuss)

My favorite dinosaur is Parasaurolophus. What made this duckbilled dinosaur different was a long, hollow tube on top of its head. Its use remains a mystery. Scientists at first thought it was used as a snorkel, but it was closed at the top. Still, when I go snorkeling I pretend I am GARY-saurolophus.

Gary

Nanosaurus (NAN-a-saw-russ)

My favorite dinosaur is Nanosaurus, which means "dwarf lizard," because it was so little, just like my cat. It was very light on its feet, just like my cat, and it was very speedy, just like my cat. If I had discovered this lively little dinosaur, I would have named it after my cat, IVAN-osaurus.

Ivan

Plateosaurus (PLAY-tee-a-saw-russ)

My favorite dinosaur is Plateosaurus. This dinosaur's name means "flat lizard" because it had flat, platelike teeth for chewing leaves. Although it sometimes ate meat, it was a vegetarian most of the time, just like me! I even love to plant my own vegetables. So it's only natural to call this dinosaur KATY-osaurus!

Katy

Erlikosaurus (er-LIK-a-saw-russ)

My favorite dinosaur is Erlikosaurus. It was unusual because of its toothless beak, sharp teeth on the sides of its jaws, and webbed toes. Scientists think it was an expert fish catcher. My dad is teaching me how to fish. I'm going to be the best fish catcher ever. Then they could call this dinosaur ERIC-osaurus.

Eric

"Supersaurus" (SOO-per-saw-russ)

My favorite dinosaur is "Supersaurus."
All that was found were a few giant bones in Colorado,
so it doesn't have an official
name yet. It may have
been even bigger than
Brachiosaurus. I'm going on
vacation to Colorado. If I
help find the rest of its
bones, they could name it
SUE-persaurus.

Sue

Dinosaurs (DIE-na-sawrs)

I don't have a favorite dinosaur,
because they are all my favorites.
I love reading about every one of them.
If I had my way, I would change their
name from dinosaurs to
DIANE-osaurs.

Diane

Think about your favorite dinosaur.
Wouldn't you like a dinosaur named after

YOU ?

Pterodactylus
ter-a-DAK-tie-luss

Ornithomimus
orn-ith-a-MY-muss

Iguanodon
ig-WAN-a-don

Plateosaurus
PLAY-tee-a-saw-russ

Microvenator
mike-row-ven-AY-tor

Apatosaurus
ah-PAT-a-saw-russ

Brontosaurus
BRON-ta-saw-russ

Brachiosaurus
BRAK-ee-a-saw-russ

Nanosaurus
NAN-a-saw-russ

Ammosaurus
AM-a-saw-russ

Dravidosaurus
dra-VID-a-saw-russ

Yaleosaurus
YALE-ee-a-saw-russ

Anodontosaurus
an-a-dont-a-SAW-russ

Avimimus
a-vee-MY-muss

Pentaceratops
PEN-ta-ser-a-tops